The big 5
and other wild animals

Rhino
Megan Emmett

The big 5 and other wild animals series is published by
Awareness Publishing Group (Pty) Ltd.
Copyright © 2019

Awareness Publishing (SA) (Pty) Ltd
www.awareness.co.za
info@awareness.co.za
+27 (0)86 110 1491
www.facebook.com/AwarenessPublishing

All rights reserved. No part of this publication may be reproduced in any form without written permission from the publisher, except by a reviewer.

First edition, 2019

Rhino by Megan Emmett
ISBN 978-0-6393-0006-1

Summary: An introduction to the white rhino, one of the Big Five wild animals. This book looks at the differences between white rhino and black rhino, the white rhino's physical characteristics and its daily activities, and its family life and territory. The book also talks about the conservation of rhinos.

Book design: Dana Espag and Bianca Keenan-Smith.

Editorial credits: Educational consultant: Gillian Mervis. Copy editor: Danya Ristić. Proofreader: Lynda Gilfillan. Picture editor: Anne Laing. Indexer: Lois C Henderson.

Illustrations: Cartoons: Gerhard Cruywagen of Greenhouse Cartoons, and Dana Espag.

Photo credits: Cover and pp.6, 7, 9, 10, 14, 16, 18, 22 (left), 24, 26, 37 (bottom), 40, 42 (top), 44, and 50 © Anne Laing; p.3 (top) © Ecoimages / Shutterstock; (middle) © Karel Gallas / Shutterstock; (bottom) © cptsai / Shutterstock; pp.4, 8, 13, 19, 22 (right), 23 (top), and 36 © Shem Compion; p.11 © Palenque / iStockphoto; pp.12, 15, 27 and 48 © Megan Emmett; p.17 © Doug Cheeseman / Gallo Images; p.20 © huibvisser / Shutterstock; p.23 (bottom) © Alamy Images / Gallo Images; p.28 © Karel Gallas / Shutterstock; p.30 (top) © Reinhard Eisele / Great Stock / Corbis; (bottom) © Alamy Images / Gallo Images; p.32 (top) © Alamy Images / Gallo Images; (bottom) © Alamy Images / AfriPics; p.34 © Alamy Images / Gallo Images; p.37 (top) GlobalP / iStockphoto; (middle) © Graeme Shannon / Shutterstock; p.38 © Alamy Images / Gallo Images; p.41 © John Warden / Gallo Images; p.42 (bottom) © Doug Cheeseman / Gallo Images; p.45 (top) © MartinMaritz / Shutterstock; (bottom) © Alamy Images / Gallo Images; p.46 © Gallo Images; p.49 © Paul Weinberg / Africa Media Online.

You can read more by Megan Emmett about animals in the book *Game Ranger in Your Backpack – All-in-one Interpretative Guide to the Lowveld*, published by Briza Publications (2010, Pretoria). ISBN 978-1-920217-06-8.

1 3 5 7 9 0 8 6 4 2

Contents

Quick facts 5
Meet the rhino 7
White and black rhino 9
The rhino's body 11
The rhino's feet 13
The rhino's horns 15
The white rhino's square mouth 17
Munch, munch, and step forward 19
Drinking water 21
Mud wallowing 23
Habits 25
Family life 27
The home range 29
Bulls' territories 31
Marking territory 33
Fighting 35
Seeing, smelling and hearing 37
Flehmen 39
Finding a mate 41
Danger and speed 43
Rhinos and birds 45
Rhino in danger 47
Saving the rhino 49
Glossary 51

The white rhino has a wide, straight lip and a large hump over its shoulders.

Quick facts

Height (at the shoulder)	1,8 metres
Weight	Male: Up to 2 400 kilograms Female: About 1 600 kilograms
Lifespan	About 40 years
Gestation (pregnancy)	16 months
Number of young	One at a time
Habitat	Flat areas with grass for feeding on, thick bush for resting in, water for drinking, and mud for wallowing
Food	White rhinos prefer short, fresh grass
Predators	Lion and hyena kill and eat rhino calves. Humans often kill adult rhinos for their horns or meat, or as a sport
Is it one of the Big Five?	Yes!

Words that appear in the text in bold, **like this**, are explained in the Glossary at the end of this book. Some key words are in colour.

"Rhino is short for rhinoceros. The word rhinoceros comes from the Greek words *rhis* meaning "nose" and *keras* meaning "horn.""

The white rhino's body is shaped like a barrel, and its tail is short and thin.

Meet the rhino

The white rhinoceros (REYE-noh-se-riss), or white rhino (REYE-noe), is the second-largest animal in Africa that lives on land. Rhinos have big barrel-shaped bodies, with a bulge in the middle. They have two sharp-tipped horns on their heads and a short, thin tail. They are not **aggressive** animals, and will not usually attack, but they can be dangerous if they are frightened.

People watching a rhino cross the road in a game reserve.

Because rhinos are such big animals that can also be dangerous, they are part of a group that we call the Big Five. The Big Five are the largest and most dangerous animals in the wild. The other animals in this group are buffalo, elephant, lion and leopard. Long ago, people from Europe used to come to Africa to hunt the Big Five, to prove and show how brave they were. Nowadays, many people go on holiday to a game reserve to see the Big Five, and rhino is one of the animals that they want to see the most.

Where might the name come from?

The story goes that white rhinos got their name from a misunderstanding of the Dutch word wijd, meaning "wide", which was translated into English as "white". The Dutch word could have described the rhino's wide mouth or the wide-open spaces where they live.

The black rhino eats the leaves, twigs and young branches of bushes. It has a pointed and hook-shaped upper lip, which helps it to grab hold of its food.

White and black rhino

There are two kinds of rhino: the white rhino and the black rhino. Their names suggest that they are different colours, but this is not true. White rhino and black rhino are both grey in colour, but there are some other differences. One difference is that white rhino are bigger than black rhino. Another difference is the shape of their lips: white rhino have a square-shaped lip, while the black rhino's lip is pointed.

White rhino and black rhino also live in different places. The white rhino likes open areas where there is lots of grass to eat. Animals that eat grass are called grazers. Black rhino do not eat grass. They live in places that have thick bush, because they eat leaves from bushes and trees. Because of this, we say that they are browsers.

This book is only about the white rhino, and not about the black rhino.

White rhinos have wide, square lips, which help them to pick and eat short grass.

The white rhino keeps its head close to the ground for eating grass and for smelling other rhino.

The rhino's body

White rhinos have a big hump on their shoulders. They also have very thick, short necks. Their strong necks hold up their large, heavy heads. White rhinos keep their heads close to the ground so that they can graze grass.

The rhino has a good sense of smell. Because the rhino's head is close to the ground when it grazes, it can smell whether other rhinos are nearby. If it smells other rhino, it will either look for those rhino or move away. Rhinos need to have a good sense of smell because their eyesight is poor.

The white rhino's short, thick neck is strong enough to hold up its big, heavy head.

The underneath part of a rhino's foot, showing its cracked skin and three toes.

The rhino's feet

Rhino have large feet to support their large bodies. On each foot there are three toes. One big toe is in the front, and there is one smaller toe on either side of the big toe.

At the back of the foot, the rhino's heel makes a "W" shape. When the rhino walks, all three toes and the W shape at the back can be seen in the rhino's footprint, or track.

The skin on the bottom of the rhino's foot is very rough and cracked. Often, the cracks are so deep that they show in the rhino's tracks.

A rhino's front footprint in the sand.

The white rhino has two horns – the longer, sharper horn is at the front of its face, and the shorter horn is higher up its face. This rhino looks as if its skin is red because it has been rolling in red sand.

The rhino's horns

Rhinos have two horns. One long horn is at the front of their faces, above their noses. Behind the long horn, closer to the eyes, is a shorter horn.

The horns are made of a hard material called keratin. We also have keratin, in our fingernails. A rhino's horns grow between two and six centimetres in a year, and they carry on growing throughout the rhino's life.

White rhino bulls use their horns to fight.

Rhinos use their horns to protect themselves and their babies from predators such as lions. Baby rhinos are called calves. Bull, or male, rhinos also use their horns when they fight with each other. A bull uses his long horn more often than a cow, or female, rhino does, and his horn gets worn down with use.

Cows' horns are usually longer and thinner than those of bulls. Because cows do not fight as often as bulls fight, their horns are not so worn down, broken or damaged. Cows' horns usually just carry on growing. The longest horn ever measured on a white rhino was 1,58 metres!

White rhinos graze by tearing the grass off at ground level with their lips.

The white rhino's square mouth

White rhino eat grass – they are grazers. They use their wide, square lips to eat the grass. Most animals use their teeth to bite and chew. White rhino use their lips to pull up large amounts of grass.

Rhinos' heads are long, and their mouths reach close to the ground. The top lip pushes the grass into the rhino's mouth. The bottom lip is hard and helps to cut grass. The rhino pulls its head upwards when it wants to cut the grass.

Rhinos have big, flat teeth called molars. We also have molars. These are the big teeth at the back of our mouths. A rhino's molars are much bigger than ours. These teeth grind and crush the grass that the rhino eats.

Eating soil and dung

Sometimes, rhinos eat soil. This is called geophagia (jee-oh-FAY-ja). "Geo" comes from a Greek word that means "earth", and phagein *is a Greek word that means "to eat". The soil has special* **minerals** *in it that rhinos need to stay healthy.*

Rhinos sometimes also eat **dung***. This is called coprophagia (cop-roh-FAY-ja), because copro comes from the Greek word* kopros*, which means "dung". Rhinos eat dung for the healthy and nutritious parts of food in it that were not completely digested.*

A rhino eats in a half-circle around its front legs, and then moves forward to eat more.

Munch, munch, and step forward

When a rhino is grazing, it stands still and moves its head in a half-circle, taking bites of grass from one side to the other. After several bites it steps forward and repeats the actions.

White rhinos have favourite places for eating. Because they visit the same area again and again, they keep the grass short. In fact, they prefer to eat grass that is short and fresh. So a rhino returns to its favourite places and, by grazing, cuts the grass down before it grows long again. But the rhino does not visit the same places too often. It does not want to eat *all* the grass that is there, because if it did there would be no grass left to eat.

Rhinos return to graze in their favourite places where the grass is good, so the grass does not have a chance to grow too long.

The water that rhinos drink every day helps to digest the food in their stomachs.

Drinking water

Rhinos need to drink lots of water, because the grass that they eat is quite dry. Water helps them to digest their food, and break the food down into tiny pieces that can be used by their bodies. Rhinos drink water every day, and sometimes twice a day. They live only in places where there is plenty of water for them to drink.

Rhinos usually drink late in the afternoon, or after dark, when the temperature is cooler.

If there is a drought and it has not rained for a long time, rhinos may not have enough water to drink. The longest that they can survive, staying alive without water, is four days.

Bulls live alone. They do not like other bull rhinos entering their area, but they will let other bulls come in when these bulls need to drink water. Water is extremely important for rhinos' survival.

Rhinos and terrapins

Sometimes, while rhinos wallow in mud, terrapins swim up to them and eat the ticks off their bodies. Terrapins are similar to tortoises, but they live in waterholes. Tortoises eat plants, while terrapins eat ticks, fish and birds.

Two terrapins enjoying the sun.

Rhinos enjoy wallowing in mud.

Mud wallowing

When animals roll around in mud, we say that they are wallowing in the mud. White rhinos enjoy wallowing because it helps them to keep cool in hot weather.

When a rhino has finished wallowing, the mud stays on its skin. The surface or top layer of the mud forms a dry crust. Under the crust, the layer of mud that is closest to the rhino's skin stays damp. This damp layer helps to keep the skin cool. The mud is also like a natural sunscreen lotion – it stops the rhino's skin from getting sunburnt.

When all the mud is completely dry, it begins to make the rhino's skin itchy. The rhino then rubs the mud off against a tree. As the rhino rubs away the mud, it also removes parasites, such as ticks. These small creatures bite the rhino's skin and suck its blood. Parasites can make an animal sick.

Usually, rhinos rub their bodies against trees, but sometimes they use rocks or piles of hard sand. They have favourite rubbing posts, which can become quite smooth from all the rubbing. Rhinos also use rubbing posts to scratch their bellies and other parts of their bodies that are hard for them to reach.

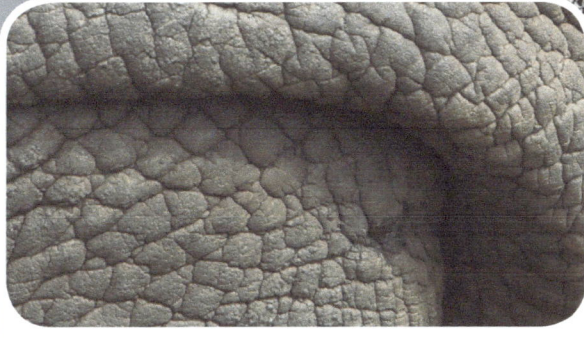

A rhino's skin is rough and thick, so it is hard for the rhino to stay cool.

A rhino rubbing its face on a tree stump, which has become smooth from all the rubbing.

Rhinos rest in the shade on hot summer days.

Habits

Rhinos have certain habits, or things that they do over and over again. They eat during the day, as they move around. Rhinos need to eat huge amounts of food to fill their big bodies. For this reason, they also eat at night. In fact, to get enough to eat, they have to spend at least half of their time feeding.

Rhinos also usually rest and sleep when it is hot, during the middle of the day. They find a shady spot under a big bush, or a sandy place such as a dry riverbed where the sand is soft. But they will sleep there only if the area is shady as well.

When rhinos sleep, they sleep deeply and breathe heavily. But even while they are asleep, their ears move all the time. A rhino picks up sounds by flicking its ears in every direction. If there is danger nearby, the rhino will hear it and quickly jump to its feet.

Rhinos do not like cold and windy weather, so they hide away in thick bushes, where they sleep until the weather gets warmer and less windy.

A mother rhino grazes while her young calf stays close to her.

Family life

Female white rhino are called cows, and they usually live together with other rhino cows and their calves. But sometimes a cow stays alone with her calf.

It takes up to four years for rhino calves to grow up. To take good care of her calf, the cow usually has only one calf with her at a time. When this calf is three or four years old, the cow may give birth to another calf. When she has a new calf, she chases away the older one and keeps the younger calf with her. The older calf may try to come back. The mother sometimes allows the older calf to stay for a while.

When young rhinos grow up and leave their mothers, they meet up with other rhinos and form groups of about five. Males and females may live together in these groups for a time.

A group of white rhino cows grazing together.

Rhinos live together in groups so that there are more eyes and ears to look out for danger.

The home range

The area that cows live in is called a **home range**. A home range is an area that a cow knows well. The cows do not defend this area – they let other rhino come into it.

Cows that do not have calves often stay together. They enjoy being with each other. They also notice danger better when they are in a group, because there are two or more pairs of eyes and ears to look and listen out for **predators**.

If there is an area with plenty of green grass and water, many rhino cows will go there. Sometimes more than ten cows drink and feed together as a group in one area.

When there is a lot of good grazing and water, a cow's home range may be as small as six square kilometres. But when the season is dry and food is hard to find, the home range may be as large as 20 square kilometres.

A younger rhino bull urinating in a long stream, to show respect to the older bull that has let the younger bull into his territory.

Male rhinos fight if the younger bull is not respectful when he enters the older bull's territory to find water.

Bulls' territories

White rhino bulls live alone. Each bull lives in his own area, or **territory**.

A male rhino becomes an adult when he is four years old. Until the males are adults, they do not have territories. Only the older, strongest bulls have territories. A bull will start to fight for a territory when he is about 12 years old.

A rhino bull defends his territory, keeping other bulls out. Bulls become angry and aggressive when other bulls enter their territories, but they do not mind if cows come in.

A bull will let other males into his territory only if they need to drink water. But these males must show respect to the older bull. The younger bulls show respect by flattening their ears or squealing. They also show respect by urinating in a long stream, which is different from the urine spray that a bull produces when marking his territory.

A bull's territory is usually small compared to a cow's home range. The territory may be as small as one square kilometre. Or it may be as big as 14 square kilometres.

A bull rhino uses rivers, streams or hills to show other rhino where his territory begins and ends. He even uses man-made roads when he marks the edges, or boundaries, of his territory.

A rhino bull spreading his dung to mark his territory.

While patrolling his territory, a bull sprays urine backwards onto the grass to mark his territory.

Marking territory

When bull rhinos walk through their territories, we say that they are patrolling the area. While patrolling, bull rhinos mark their territories, showing other rhinos where the territory begins and ends. A bull rhino marks his territory by leaving smells behind and by making certain signs.

To leave smells behind, bull rhinos give off their waste matter by defecating and urinating. They make big piles of their dung, called middens. Every time they walk past a midden on their patrols, they add dung to the pile, so middens can become large. Cows and young bulls also add their dung to a bull's midden, but they do not break up their balls of dung as bull rhinos do. When the owner of the midden walks past it again, he can smell who has visited his area.

A bull rhino kicks his dung, so that he will carry the smell of the dung on his feet. He leaves this smell behind as he walks around his territory. Bulls also spray urine on the ground, on bushes or on rocks. They scrape their feet where they urinate and, as with their dung, the smell stays on their feet. The smell also remains on the ground where they have walked.

To make a sign, bulls scrape their back feet in the sand. When other bulls see these scrape marks on the ground, they know that the territory belongs to another bull.

When bulls fight, they try to stab each other with their horns.

Fighting

While a rhino bull is patrolling the boundaries and edges of his territory, he sometimes meets another bull. When this happens, the bulls do not always fight. The bull shows off to his neighbour by standing still and snorting. The neighbour may be **impressed** with the bull's behaviour and move off.

If a bull rhino is old enough to have a territory, he will be prepared to fight with another bull to get that territory. Bull rhinos also fight over a cow that is ready to mate.

Bull rhinos fight with their horns. They use their horns in the same way that people use spears or knives for fighting. They try to stab each other with their horns.

The skin on a rhino's shoulders is about 2,5 centimetres thick and helps to protect the rhino from his enemy's horns. Rhino horns are hard and sharp. They can cause injuries that may bleed. Sometimes, one of the bulls may even die during a fight.

Cows only fight with predators, such as lions, to protect their calves.

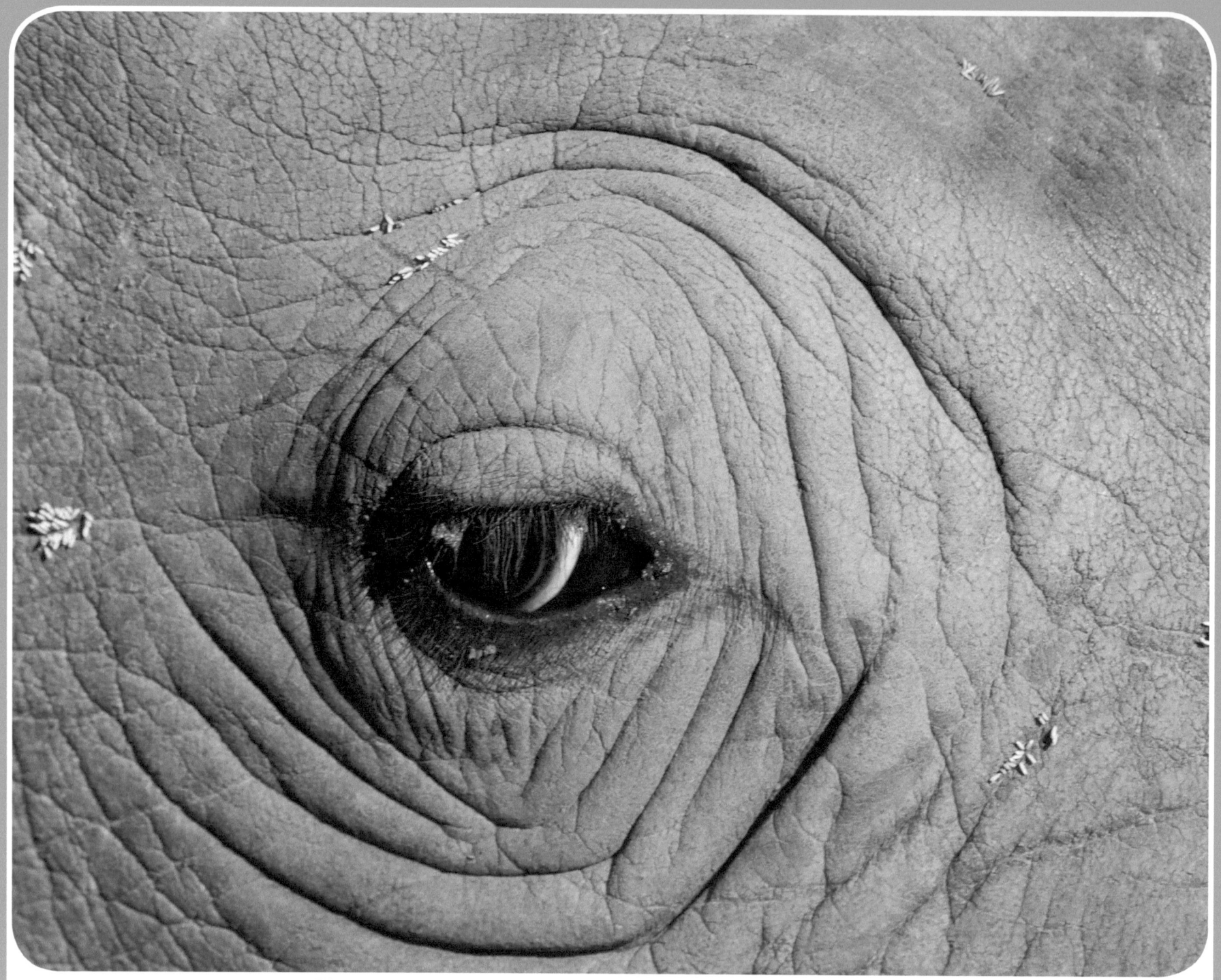
Rhinos cannot see very well, unless the thing is close by.

Seeing, smelling and hearing

Rhinos have poor eyesight. They can only see well when things are close by. They can see things that are further away, but it is usually when something moves that they notice it. A movement in the distance warns the rhino that there may be danger.

A rhino's hearing and sense of smell are extremely good. Rhinos find food, and each other, by smelling. The smell of a rhino remains on the ground where it has walked. A bull stays away from other bulls' territories when he smells the dung or urine of the other bulls on the ground. A calf knows its mother by her smell.

A rhino's ears are on the top of its head. This is so that the rhino can still hear when its head is close to the ground. While the rhino is grazing, its ears move all the time, in every direction, to listen for sounds. When the rhino hears a sound, both its ears point in the direction of the sound to find out what it is.

A rhino bull pulling up his top lip – he is doing the flehmen test to see if a nearby female is ready to mate.

Flehmen

When a cow rhino is ready to mate, we say that she is in heat, or in **oestrus** (EE-striss). Rhino bulls find out if a cow is ready to mate by doing a test called flehmen (FLE-men). Flehmen is a way by which some animals use the top of their mouth to detect and discover smells left by other animals. The word comes from the German word *flehmen*, which means "curling up the upper lip".

The bull does flehmen by smelling the urine, or waste matter, that the cow urinates as she walks through the bull's territory. Then the bull pulls up his lip. When he lifts his lip, a small hole or gland on the roof of his mouth opens. The gland picks up the smell of the chemicals in the cow's urine. These chemicals tell the bull if the cow is ready to mate or not.

A female rhino, on the left, charges at a male who wants to mate with her.

Finding a mate

If a bull finds a cow that is in oestrus and is ready to mate, he tries to keep her in his territory for as long as possible. He herds her, like a sheepdog herds sheep. He chases her if she tries to leave. The bull even clashes horns with the cow to keep her in his territory. During this time, the bull makes lots of noise, squealing and snorting loudly.

A cow does not always want to mate. She may charge at the bull, or even fight with him. Sometimes, she leaves one bull's territory and enters another bull's territory. But if the cow wants to mate with the bull, she stays with him in his territory. They may stay together for two or even three weeks. When they mate, it takes a long time, often more than half an hour.

Two rhino preparing to mate.

This rhino is scared – its tail is curled over, and it is running across the road to hide in the bush.

A cow rhino making sure that her calf stays nearby, where she can see it.

Danger and speed

A group of rhinos is usually called a herd of rhino. We sometimes also say a crash of rhino because this describes the crashing sound that these animals make when they run through the bush.

Rhinos are big and heavy, but they can move quickly and easily. If they need to, rhino can charge at an enemy at a speed of 40 kilometres per hour. That means that they can run across ten metres of ground in less than a second!

If a rhino is scared, it curls its tail up in a circle. Sometimes, a rhino moves or bounces around on one spot. This shows that it is afraid of a predator or another rhino. The rhino turns sideways to show the enemy how big he is. If this has no effect, he may rub his horn on the ground to scare the enemy off.

Rhino cows are very protective of their calves. When a cow and her calf run away from danger, the calf always runs ahead of its mother. This way, the mother can see where her calf is so that she can protect it.

Red-billed oxpeckers eating ticks off a rhino's back.

Rhinos and birds

When rhinos are grazing or resting in the bush, small brown birds often sit on their backs. These birds are called oxpeckers, and there are two types. Red-billed oxpeckers have completely red beaks. Yellow-billed oxpeckers have some red and some yellow on their beaks.

Oxpeckers eat the ticks that are on a rhino's skin. Ticks are parasites that bite through the rhino's skin and suck its blood. By dealing with the ticks, oxpeckers and rhinos help each other: the rhinos are clean and are free of ticks, and the oxpeckers have a meal.

Because rhinos cannot see well, the oxpeckers also help to warn rhinos of danger. When the birds are disturbed by a predator they fly away, making a lot of noise. The hissing and rasping noise tells rhinos that a predator is nearby. The noise also tells humans that there are rhino close by.

Sometimes, white birds walk through the grass near rhinos. These birds are larger than oxpeckers, and they are called cattle egrets (EE-grits). They eat the insects that are kicked up by the rhino's feet when it walks in the grass.

A cattle egret walks near a rhino hoping to find some insects that the rhino may have kicked up in the grass.

A red-billed oxpecker sitting on a rhino's horn.

An investigator checks the bones and skin of a rhino that was killed by poachers in the Kruger National Park. The coloured flags and numbers mark important clues and information about the poachers.

Rhino in danger

The black rhino is one of Africa's top ten most **endangered** animals. Very few black rhino are left in Africa or in other places in the world where they live. White rhino are also endangered, but there are more white than black rhino alive nowadays.

Most rhinos are found in Africa, in countries such as South Africa, Namibia, Botswana, Zimbabwe, Zambia, Kenya and Tanzania. There are also some rhinos in Asian countries such as India, Nepal and Indonesia.

Some people kill rhinos to cut off and sell the animals' horns. In countries such as China and Vietnam, people buy rhino horn to show that they are wealthy and use rhino horns for medicine. They believe that rhino horn can make people strong and cure illnesses.

Because white rhino are also in danger of dying out, there may come a time when there are no more rhino left in the bush. If this happens, smaller animals such as wildebeest and zebra will suffer. Like elephants and hippos, white rhinos open up the bush while walking through it. They trample the bush, crushing it under their heavy feet. This makes it easier for the other, smaller animals to come and graze after them. And these animals eat the short, soft grass that the rhinos have left behind.

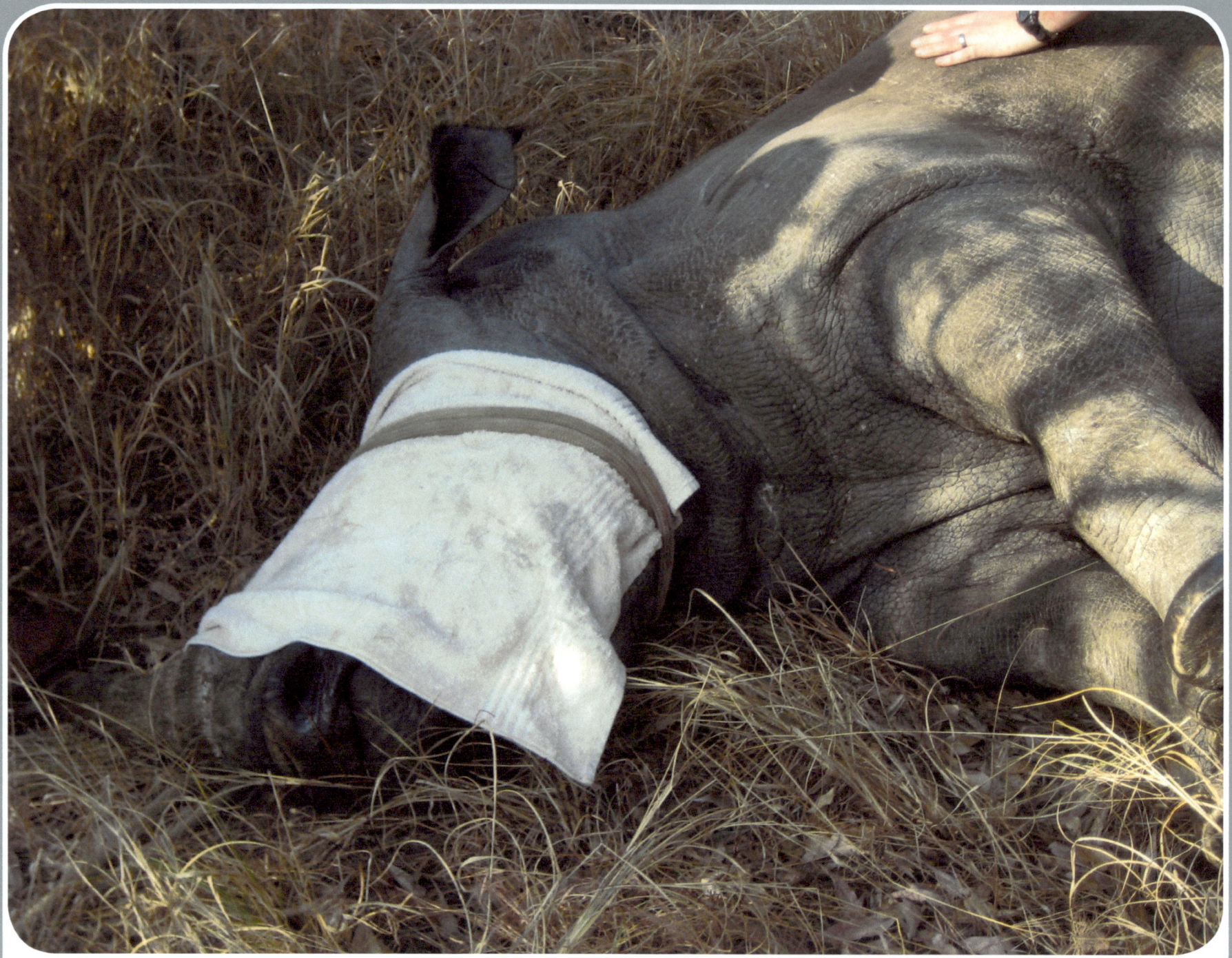

This rhino has been drugged and made to sleep so that it can be checked and then moved to a new game reserve.

Saving the rhino

In the 1950s and 1960s, there were just a few black and white rhino left in South Africa. Many rhino had been killed by **poachers** who wanted to sell the horns. Dr Ian Player was the warden in charge of the Imfolozi Game Reserve in KwaZulu-Natal. He was very worried that so few rhino survived, and so he started a project called "Operation Rhino".

Many people joined Dr Player in Operation Rhino to help protect the rhinos in the Imfolozi reserve. They stopped the poachers from killing the rhinos, and over time, the number of rhinos grew. The team from Operation Rhino moved some of the rhino to other game reserves in South Africa, where the rhino were protected and where rhino calves were born. South Africa is now famous around the world for saving the rhino from becoming **extinct**.

Nowadays, South Africa has the biggest number of white and black rhinos in the world. But we need to make sure that we continue to keep rhino safe, because poachers still kill rhinos for their horns. Almost 700 rhinos were killed in South Africa in 2012.

Dr Ian Player, who started the Operation Rhino project at the Imfolozi Game Reserve in the 1960s.

The white rhino has two horns. The front horn is longer and is used to fight with other rhino.

Glossary

aggressive – likely to attack

browsers – animals that eat the leaves of bushes and trees

dung – an animal's solid waste matter

endangered – wild animals that are in danger of dying out and not existing any longer

extinct – no longer living in the wild

grazers – animals that eat grass

home range – the area where animals live and feed

impressed – to take notice of, or to be frightened by

minerals – substances or matter found in nature that can help to keep living creatures healthy

oestrus – the times when a female is ready to mate

poachers – people who break the law by stealing and killing animals for food or to sell their body parts

predators – animals that hunt and kill other animals for food

territory – the specific area where only one male rhino lives

www.ingramcontent.com/pod-product-compliance
Lightning Source LLC
Chambersburg PA
CBHW041322290426

44108CB00004B/108